Welcome to the world of hummingbirds!

Robert A. Tyrrell

Esther Tyrrell

Hummingbirds

JEWELS IN THE SKY

by ESTHER QUESADA TYRRELL   *photographs by* ROBERT A. TYRRELL

CROWN PUBLISHERS, INC. • *New York*

◀ ▼ *Bee hummingbird.*

There are many jewels in nature, but perhaps the most beautiful are those that fly— hummingbirds.

Hummingbirds are the smallest of all birds. But they belong to a large family. There are over 300 different kinds. The largest is the giant hummingbird. It lives in South America and is about eight and a half inches long. The smallest is the bee hummingbird. It lives in Cuba and measures a little more than two inches from the tip of its bill to the tip of its tail.

Hummingbirds are found only in the Western Hemisphere, from Alaska to the southern tip of Chile. They are very adaptable and can live in any kind of climate, whether cold or hot, very dry or humid. They thrive in swamps, jungles, and pine forests, on snow peaks, and even in deserts.

They share their habitats with animals like snakes, vultures, bats, and crocodiles.

Most hummingbirds live near the equator. Because the flowers from which they feed grow year-round, these hummers do not have to "migrate," or fly to areas where there is food.

But some hummingbirds, such as most of those that live in the United States, must migrate great distances in the winter to areas where there is adequate food and a warmer climate.

Hummingbirds are known as "flying jewels" because their feathers glitter like polished gems. In fact, there is a hummingbird named for every jewel in existence. In zoos throughout the world, hummingbird aviaries are called "jewel rooms."

Their feathers shine brilliantly because they are different from those of most other birds. They are "iridescent," and the colors are the result of a process called "interference." It is the same process that makes colors appear in a soap bubble.

The hummingbird's feathers are made up of very small air bubbles with dark spaces in between. Light bouncing off the bubbles at different angles appears as different colors. The thickness of the bubble and the amount of air inside determines the specific color of the feather.

▲ *Ruby-throated hummingbird.*

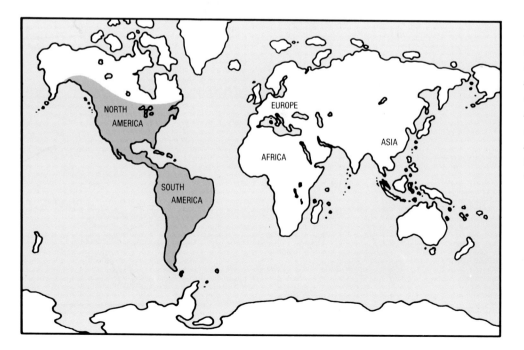

Hummingbird habitat

Hummingbirds live as far north as southern Alaska and Nova Scotia in North America, and throughout South America and the islands of the Caribbean.

▲ *Antillean crested hummingbird.*

Some hummingbirds sparkle like emeralds, rubies, and sapphires. Some have satiny wings, velvety black underparts, shimmering crests, striped tails, and shiny throats.

The male hummingbird's glittery feathers attract the attention of the female when he wishes to mate with her. They sparkle and glisten best in the sun. Most females are duller than the males of the same species so that they are safely camouflaged during the nesting season.

▼ *Purple-throated carib.*

▼ *Bahama woodstar.*

As a rule, hummingbirds that live in sunny habitats have the brightest, most sparkling feathers. But some species live in the darker parts of jungles and forests, where the sun never shines. These birds have drab feathers, and for this reason they are called "hermits." One example is the rufous-breasted hermit.

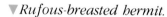 *Rufous-breasted hermit.*

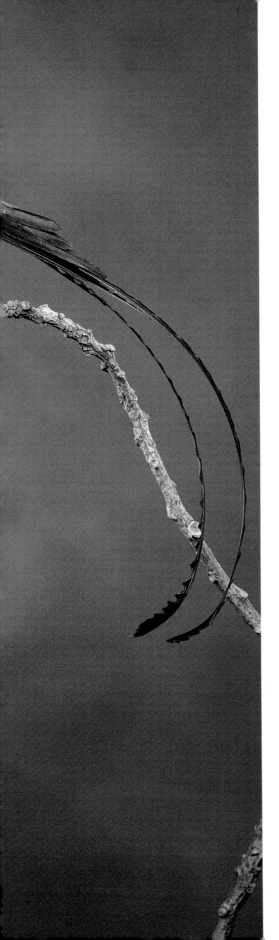

▲ *Anna's hummingbird,
hovering as it feeds.*

Because they have the best flight ability of all birds, hummingbirds are sometimes called "nature's helicopters." Every bird can fly forward, but hummingbirds can also fly backward, to the right, to the left, and straight up. They can even fly upside down!

They can also remain airborne in one spot for a long period of time. This is called "hovering." Their rapid wingbeat enables them to do this.

Green-throated carib ("el zumbador").

The hummingbird's wings beat an average of 78 times every second. But sometimes they will perform aerial dives or swoops, and then the wings will beat up to 200 times a second!

If you stand near a hummingbird, you will hear its wings making a whirring, or humming, noise. In fact, that is how the bird got its name. Early English colonists thought the wings sounded like the humming of a spinning wheel. When people from other countries named the bird, they also tried to imitate the sound of its wings. For example, Puerto Ricans call the green-throated carib *el zumbador.* In the Dominican Republic, hummingbirds are known as *zumbaflores.* Cubans refer to them as *zunzúnes.*

Its wings are so powerful that there is no need for the hummingbird to walk. For this reason, its legs are very small and weak and almost useless for anything except perching. Even if the bird must move only one inch, it will probably fly.

▼Bahama woodstar.

The hummingbird's heart is the largest, in relation to its body size, of any animal on earth. Because it is so active, the hummingbird burns energy at a very fast rate. It needs a large heart to deliver energy to its muscles quickly. When resting, the heart beats an average of 500 times a minute. If the bird becomes frightened, the heartbeat can rise to over 1,200 times a minute.

▲ *Bahama woodstar.*

Hummingbirds burn up so much energy that they must eat every 15 minutes. Their diet consists of insects and nectar. If a human being burned energy as fast as a hummingbird, he or she would have to eat 155,000 calories a day. That is equal to 285 pounds of hamburger, 370 pounds of potatoes, or 130 pounds of bread. The hummingbird will often eat up to 50 percent of its weight in nectar in a day.

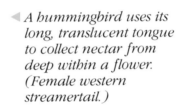

◄ A hummingbird uses its long, translucent tongue to collect nectar from deep within a flower. (Female western streamertail.)

Nectar is a sweet syrup that is found at the base of certain flowers. The flowers that the hummingbird feeds from are usually long and trumpet-shaped. The hummingbird collects the nectar by reaching into the flower with its long, narrow bill.

Many people believe that the hummingbird sucks nectar through its beak, as if it were a straw. But it is really the tongue that collects the nectar, with a licking motion like a kitten's. Hummingbirds lick very fast— about 13 licks per second.

The hummingbird's tongue is very long. By extending it, the hummingbird is able to reach nectar deep inside a flower.

The hummingbird's main source of food is nectar, which supplies it with quick energy. But the hummingbird must supplement its diet with tiny insects, which provide protein, minerals, vitamins, and fats. Sometimes you can see it hunting for insects along a roof or tree trunk. It will also fly into swarms of tiny flies or gnats and twirl around in the air as it snaps them up one by one.

The hummingbird feeds most often in the early morning and late afternoon. It is important for it to eat as much as possible at sunset so that it can store enough energy to pass the night without eating. But sometimes the bird doesn't get enough to eat, and it goes into a coma-like state called "torpor."

When a bird is in torpor, it fluffs out its feathers and lowers its temperature and its heart and breathing rates. Some reptiles, rodents, and bats also go into torpor. A torpid hummingbird can be awakened by a sound, touch, or bright light. It can take the bird over an hour to fully awaken.

▶ *Puerto Rican emerald in a coma-like state called torpor.*

Flowers provide a plentiful source of food for the hummingbird. In return, the hummingbird helps flowers reproduce. In order for plants to reproduce, pollen must be transferred from flower to flower. When a hummingbird inserts its bill into a tubular flower, powdery yellow pollen sticks to its bill, head, or breast. The pollen is then transferred to other plants as the bird travels from blossom to blossom.

▶ *Anna's hummingbird with yellow pollen grains stuck to its bill and head.*

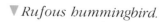

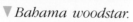

▼ *Costa's hummingbird.*

▼ *Western streamertail.*

Most of the flowers that the hummingbird selects to feed from are red, orange, or yellow. These colors do not attract the insects that might otherwise compete with hummingbirds for nectar. The flowers are also usually odorless, since the bird's sense of smell is limited.

Red flowers are the hummingbird's favorite because it knows that red flowers usually have the most generous supply of nectar. The hummingbird is so attracted to this color that it will often investigate anything red, like a hat, shirt, and even red nail polish and lipstick!

Thick petals that are not easily damaged by the bird's sturdy beak are another feature of some of the flowers hummingbirds feed from. In fact, some blooms even have shallow grooves inside to guide the bill away from their delicate interiors. Since hummingbirds can hover, there are usually no branches for perching, and the blossoms are usually arranged far apart to keep the bird's wings from becoming entangled.

These special plants generally bloom during the day when hummingbirds are active. They stay in bloom longer than other flowers that attract insects.

Although hummingbirds can hover, they sometimes prefer to sit on a petal while feeding, perhaps to save a little energy. And there are some hummers that use a shortcut to get at the nectar by poking a little hole in the base of the flower.

▲ *Blue-throated hummingbird.*

Hummingbirds do not live or travel in flocks. Because they are solitary, they are on their own when it comes to searching for food, and they are always on the lookout for sources of nectar.

Once a hummingbird has picked out a particularly good food source, such as a bush or tree with lots of flowers, it will perch on a high branch or telephone wire and begin to sing. Hummingbirds do not have very pretty voices. In fact, the voices of some species, like the Anna's hummingbird, sound like the scraping of a nail on a tin can. This song is a warning to other hummingbirds to stay away. The high position provides an excellent point from which to guard the territory against invaders.

If another bird comes near, the owner may fluff up its feathers to appear bigger, spread out its tail, and toss its shimmering head back and forth in anger.

However, there are some fearless hummingbirds that will trespass on another's territory despite these warnings. This invasion usually ends in a high-speed chase, followed by a fight.

The owner of a territory will chase and attack any creature that dares to get near its food source, regardless of its size. Cats, butterflies, and insects like bees, wasps, and yellow jackets will be attacked, as will much larger birds. We've even seen hummingbirds fight vultures hundreds of times bigger than themselves!

▶ *This ruby-throated hummingbird spreads its tail and tosses its head back and forth to signal its anger.*

Sometimes a hummingbird will use its bill to try to pierce its enemy's eyes. But usually hummingbirds rely on their sharp claws to pull out feathers and to rake each other with. Sometimes the claws lock, and then both birds fall to the ground.

▶ *Fighting ruby-throated hummingbirds.*

▼ *In this picture of two vervain hummingbirds, the sitting bird defends his perch from an intruder.*

A male hummingbird fights more during the breeding season than at any other time. During this period, he will perform dives in the air to show the female that he wishes to mate with her. But unlike some species of birds, which remain with their mates during the nesting season or even for life, hummingbirds stay together only for the few seconds it takes to mate. Then the female flies back to her nest.

This diagram shows the courtship dives performed by the male Allen's hummingbird. He makes a series of arcs 20 to 30 feet above the female, pausing and quivering at the end of each arc with his tail outspread. Then he winds his way slowly upward to a point 75 to 100 feet in the air and dives down over the female. As he dives, his feathers make a trilling sound.

The hummingbird's nest is the size of a doll's teacup and is made mainly of cobwebs. Each species makes its own special type of nest. Sometimes there are lichens, leaves, and even animal fur added. Some look like cotton candy. Some are fastened to twigs or branches and others to banana leaves. Females may also decorate them with pieces of bark.

▼ *Nesting Xantus' hummingbird.*

▶ *Nest of the bee hummingbird.*

▶▶ *Nest of the green-throated carib.*

▼ *A hummingbird egg next to a chicken's egg.*

It is the smallest bird's nest in the world, and it holds the world's smallest bird's egg. The egg is white and the size of a coffee bean. The female lays two eggs in her nest.

▶ *Purple-throated carib incubating her eggs.*

▶▶ *Baby Costa's hummingbirds.*

▶ *Anna's hummingbird feeding her chicks.*

▶▶ *Black-chinned hummingbird with chicks.*

▲ Anna's hummingbird with chicks.

The mother sits on her eggs for 15 to 22 days before they hatch. During this time she turns them with her bill or feet. When the eggs hatch, the baby birds, called "nestlings," have almost no feathers. The mother feeds them nectar and insects two or three times every hour.

Baby hummers remain in their nests for around 21 days before they "fledge," or leave the nest. Their mothers continue to feed them for many days after they have left the nest.

▶ *Young male white-eared hummingbird.*

▶ *Adult male white-eared hummingbird.*

Fledglings look different from adults. Young male hummingbirds are often mistaken for adult females because their feathers are also dull and gray. It takes several months for young male birds to acquire the brilliant adult plumage.

The hummingbird has many enemies. Among them are larger birds, like hawks, kestrels, roadrunners, and orioles. There are even some spiders and large insects, such as dragonflies and praying mantises, that will prey on hummingbirds. Hummingbird mothers are not afraid to protect their nests against crows, chipmunks, scrub jays, snakes, and yellow jackets who try to eat the eggs and nestlings. In jungles, reptiles like the giant anole prey on hummingbirds.

▲ *Anna's hummingbird.*
Legends of the Cherokee
Indians often tell how
the hummingbird
introduced them to
tobacco.

Christopher Columbus and his men were the first Europeans to see hummingbirds. The bird was important to the Native Americans who lived in the New World—so important that it was forbidden by many tribes to kill or eat one.

The Aztec Indians used hummingbird feathers to decorate the long robes of their leaders. Their god of war was named "Huitzilopochtli" (WEE-tsee-low-POACH-t'lee). *Huitzil* means "hummingbird" and *opochtli* means "sorcerer that spits fire." It was believed by the Aztecs that warriors who died in battle would be changed into glittering hummingbirds.

The hummingbird was also important to the Hopi Indians. The Hopi word for hummingbird is *totcha*. They believed that it was a powerful spirit that was sent by the sun to teach them how to make fire.

The Tewa Indians admired the bird's quick flight and often decorated their sticks with hummingbird feathers in the belief that this would help them travel faster. And Cherokee Indians believed that it was the hummingbird that first brought tobacco to their people.

▲ *This Hopi Indian "kachina" doll was used in religious ceremonies to represent Totcha, the hummingbird spirit. A kachina is an intermediary between man and a higher force. A kachina doll is a representation of this spirit.*

In Jamaica, the hummingbird is called the "doctor bird." Some say this is because the black crest and long tails of the western streamertail remind them of the top hats and long-tailed coats worn by doctors long ago. Others believe that ancient tribal doctors used hummingbirds to cure illness.

It is the national bird of Jamaica and appears often on advertisements, stamps, and paper currency and coins throughout that island.

In Puerto Rico, there is a curious folk remedy involving hummingbirds. Some people believe that the nest of the Puerto Rican emerald is useful for healing people who have asthma. They burn the nest and make a tea out of the ashes, which is then served to the sick person. Sometimes the nest is worn like a necklace instead. Many also believe that the cottony nest is a cure for an earache.

▶ *Puerto Rican emerald on her nest.*

In countries where the rain forests in which they live are not protected, some hummingbird species are in danger of becoming extinct. The forests are cut down to create areas for planting crops and grazing cattle. Some trees are made into charcoal for fuel. If the flowers in these forests disappear, the hummingbirds will have no food, and they will disappear too.

Fortunately, some countries are making an effort to protect hummingbirds. A few do this by educating their citizens about the importance of birds to the environment. When people understand the role birds play in nature, they are sometimes more careful to preserve the forest.

Other countries, like Cuba, forbid people from entering the bird's natural habitat so that it can live and thrive without danger.

Our world would be a little duller without hummingbirds. For they really are a wonderful gift from nature—tiny birds that sparkle and glitter in the air like precious jewels.

How to Attract Hummingbirds

▲ *Ruby-throated hummingbird.*

It's easy to attract hummingbirds to your backyard or balcony. The best way is to use an inexpensive feeder, which you can buy at a pet shop, nursery, or supermarket.

Fill it with a solution of four parts water to one part sugar. Never use honey or a sugar substitute, because it will harm the hummingbird.

Ask an adult to help you boil the water and then dissolve the sugar into it. Wait for the solution to cool and then fill the feeder with it. Hang the feeder in a sunny spot.

Once a week, or more often if the weather is very hot, clean the feeder out very carefully. It's best to soak it in a bucket of soapy water to which a tablespoon of bleach has been added. Scrub well and be sure to rinse it thoroughly.

Since most feeders are red, it isn't necessary to add red food coloring to the sugar solution. To discourage ants, coat the wire from which the feeder is hanging with petroleum jelly.

Now sit back and wait for one of nature's flying jewels to visit your home.

▲ *Hummingbird feeders.*

Hummingbirds of the United States

There are 16 species of hummingbird that nest in the United States. The most common are the Allen's hummingbird, the Anna's hummingbird, the black-chinned hummingbird, the broad-tailed hummingbird, the calliope hummingbird, the Costa's hummingbird, the ruby-throated hummingbird, and the rufous hummingbird. Below is a list of all 16 species, indicating where in the United States they live.

ALLEN'S HUMMINGBIRD
Size: About 3¼ inches
Plumage: *Male:* Green back. Reddish brown sides, rump, and tail. Glittering coppery throat. *Female:* Green back. Dull white underparts. Light reddish brown sides. Some metallic copper feathers scattered on the throat. **U.S. range:** Along the coast of California; occasionally Arizona, Oregon, and Washington.

ANNA'S HUMMINGBIRD ▲
Size: 3¾ inches
Plumage: *Male:* Green back. Gray underparts. Brilliant red helmet. *Female:* Dark green upperparts. Dark gray underparts with a few red feathers on the throat. **U.S. range:** California; occasionally in winter to Arizona.

BERYLLINE HUMMINGBIRD
Size: 3½ inches
Plumage: *Male:* Green and brown back. Purple-brown rump and tail. Gray or brown abdomen. Shiny green head and chest. *Female:* Similar except for less green on the abdomen. **U.S. range:** Southeast Arizona.

BLACK-CHINNED HUMMINGBIRD ▲
Size: About 3½ inches
Plumage: *Male:* Green back. Purple-bronze tail. Gray underparts. Black head and chin. Its white collar is separated from the black chin by a glittering band of violet. *Female:* Green back and head. Gray underparts. There may be a small patch of purple feathers on the throat. **U.S. range:** Western United States.

BLUE-THROATED HUMMINGBIRD
Size: About 5 inches
Plumage: *Male:* Gray-green back and head. Dull brown chest. Light blue throat. There are white eye stripes on the face and white tips on the tail. *Female:* Similar to the male except there is no blue on the throat. **U.S. range:** Parts of Arizona, New Mexico, and Texas.

BROAD-BILLED HUMMINGBIRD
Size: About 3½ inches
Plumage: *Male:* Green back. Forked blue-black tail. White underparts, green breast, and glittering blue-green throat. Bill is red with dark tip. *Female:* Green back. Gray breast and underparts. Same red bill with dark tip. **U.S. range:** Southern Arizona.

BROAD-TAILED HUMMINGBIRD ▼
Size: About 4 inches
Plumage: *Male:* Green back, head, and upperparts. Brilliant rose red throat. Dull gray underparts. *Female:* Green upperparts. Dull brownish gray underparts. **U.S. range:** Western United States.

BUFF-BELLIED HUMMINGBIRD

Size: 4 inches

Plumage: *Males and females are identical.* Green back and crown. Brilliant green throat. Light brown underparts. Reddish bill. **U.S. range:** Coastal regions of southern Texas.

CALLIOPE HUMMINGBIRD ▶

Size: About 3 inches. *This is the smallest bird in the United States.*

Plumage: *Male:* Gold-green back. Gray underparts. Long purple feathers extend across its white throat. *Female:* Greenish upperparts. Pale gray underparts. **U.S. range:** Western United States.

COSTA'S HUMMINGBIRD ▲

Size: About 3 inches

Plumage: *Male:* Green back. Light gray underparts. Green upperparts. Shiny purple helmet that extends out along the sides. *Female:* Greenish bronze upperparts. Pale gray underparts. **U.S. range:** Southwestern United States.

LUCIFER HUMMINGBIRD

Size: 3¾ inches

Plumage: *Male:* Green back. Gray underparts. Gray-green head. Brilliant purple throat. Bill curved downward. *Female:* Green upperparts. Pale gray underparts. **U.S. range:** Occasionally in southwestern Arizona, New Mexico, and Texas.

MAGNIFICENT HUMMINGBIRD

Size: About 4½ inches

Plumage: *Male:* Green upperparts. Purple head, green throat, and green-black breast. *Female:* Green upperparts. Gray underparts. **U.S. range:** Southern New Mexico and Arizona.

RUBY-THROATED HUMMINGBIRD ▲

Size: About 3½ inches

Plumage: *Male:* Green back and grayish underparts. Green head. Bright red throat. *Female:* Similar to the male except for the absence of the red throat. There are also white spots on the tail. **U.S. range:** Eastern United States.

RUFOUS HUMMINGBIRD ▲

Size: About 3½ inches

Plumage: *Male:* Reddish brown back. White breast. Light brown underparts. Metallic copper throat. *Female:* Green back. Dull white underparts. There are sometimes a few coppery feathers on the throat. **U.S. range:** Western United States.

VIOLET-CROWNED HUMMINGBIRD

Size: About 4 inches

Plumage: *Male:* Gray-brown back. White throat and underparts. Bright violet-blue head. Red bill with black tip. *Female:* Same as the male except that her feathers are duller. **U.S. range:** Southeastern Arizona and southwestern New Mexico.

WHITE-EARED HUMMINGBIRD

Size: 3½ inches

Plumage: *Male:* Greenish gold back. Green and white abdomen. Violet head with a broad white stripe behind the eye. Violet and emerald green throat. Red bill with a black tip. *Female:* Similar to the male except that her head is brown and she has pale gray underparts. **U.S. range:** Southeastern Arizona.

Index

About the Authors

Esther and Robert Tyrrell are a husband-and-wife team of adventurers who have studied hummingbirds for 16 years. They have traveled over 80,000 miles through some of the world's most dangerous jungles and swamps to look for them. They have written two books—*Hummingbirds: Their Life and Behavior* and *Hummingbirds of the Caribbean.* Their work has appeared in *National Geographic, Natural History* magazine, and both *National Wildlife* and *International Wildlife.* They have presented their popular hummingbird show at museums and zoos throughout the United States. Esther and Robert Tyrrell live in El Monte, California. This is their first book for children.

*This book is dedicated to you,
the young reader, with love.*

Published by Crown Publishers, Inc., a Random House company, 201 East 50th Street, New York, New York 10022
CROWN is a trademark of Crown Publishers, Inc.
Manufactured in Hong Kong
Library of Congress Cataloging-in-Publication Data
Tyrrell, Esther Quesada.
　Hummingbirds : jewels in the sky / by Esther Quesada Tyrrell ;
photographs by Robert A. Tyrrell.
　　p.　cm.
　Summary: Text and photographs introduce the physical characteristics and behavior of several species of hummingbirds.
　1. Hummingbirds—Juvenile literature.　[1. Hummingbirds.]　I. Tyrrell, Robert A., ill.　II. Title.
　QL696.A558T85　1992
　598'.899—dc20　　　　　　　　　　　　　　　　　　　　　91-40857
ISBN 0-517-58390-9 (trade)
ISBN 0-517-58391-7 (lib. bdg.)
10 9 8 7 6 5 4 3